ECHOES

JEAN MÉZIÈRE

ECHOES

A VISION OF
THE AMERICAN
SOUTHWEST

TAYLOR PUBLISHING COMPANY
DALLAS, TEXAS

778.936

Book designed by Montfort Concept and Design.

Library of Congress Cataloging-in-Publication Data

Mézière, Jean.
  Echoes : a vision of the American Southwest.

  1. Photography — Southwest, New — Landscapes.
2. Southwest, New — Pictorial works. 3. Deserts —
Southwest, New — Pictorial works. I. Title.
TR660.5.M48   1986   779'.092'4   86-5964
ISBN 0-87833-525-0

Printed in the United States of America

TO LYNNE AND JEAN

INTRODUCTION

It all began with words: New Mexico, Arizona, Utah, Nevada. Key words open doors onto dreamlike spaces. Incantations carry the promise of an *elsewhere*, of a purity in which experience is revelation, light illumination, and the slightest image a vision. These words, their magic and their mystery resonate in Jean Mézière's soul — a universal summons toward territories where nature and imagination contest geographic limits.

In these landscapes at the beginning — or the end — of the world, in these white sand deserts and wind-scored canyons, everything is artistically possible. The dust and winds of sand have irrevocably swept away man and his traces, reducing him to a passing whimsy that is gone as soon as it becomes real, like a ghost town. The artist is offered a *tabula rasa*. "There is too much space there to think," says Mézière. "I let my senses go and don't try to control my aestheticism." The desert reinvents man, takes him back to his origins. These primordial lands silhouette new spaces of freedom, and for Mézière "there can be expression only to the extent that there is freedom."

In the sierras of New Mexico, Death Valley, or the Mojave Desert, lands of utmost solitude where man's traces seldom survive, the conflict of scale, a conflict between mutability and the spectacle of geological eternity, explodes into a stark reality. As Gertrude Stein would say, "When you get there, there's no there there." The landscape spreads out in a cinemascope, offering the formidable challenge of unlimited photographic freedom. Mézière forgets his frame of reference and his cultural orientation in order to let himself flow in the order of things. Osmotically, the space assimilates the photographer and the man assimilates the space. "You feel gauche. You arrive with your rules, to meet a landscape whose rules are of another dimension. These are the only places in the world where I've seen a space which nourishes itself, with nothing which can diminish it." It is up to the photographer to attempt the integration, or at least the taming, of this dimension. Under the high suns and in the band of dust, it is up to him to find his center of gravity in the plenitude and chaos.

The photographer is the lookout in these seas of sand that the mesas puncture like the bows of ships. He sees from afar a ribbon of snow between the peaks, a passing cloud, a verdant thicket in an arid wash, the mirages—phantom images that shimmer under the sun and then dissolve. The landscape is fluid, enveloping, with no beginning or end. It flees when the eye tries to inscribe it within the limited, arbitrary rectangle of a camera.

Photography is judgment — selection and exclusion at the same time. It carves the frame of an artistic desire within space, eliminating all but the subject. But the desert resists this reductive game in which eternity would be expressed on 35-millimeter film. *Everything* is the subject, and no specific image can be dissociated from the All. The challenge is to reap the instantaneous, the snapshot, from this eternity. "Where is the point of departure?" Mézière asks himself. He is at the foot of these natural monuments, of these screens through which man can catch a glimpse of genesis. He sees "the paradox of photography which is a simple act, and of a total and captivating comprehension," trying to inscribe the one within the other.

In the uncertainty of the desert, the camera ceases to be an "objective" instrument which slices space into representative portions. The machine is frozen. It flirts at the limits of the real and the unreal, where sight becomes vision and the photog-

rapher, carried away by the rush of the desert, becomes a visionary. Along with poetry, photography is an art which allows the artist to sail in a state of hyper-receptivity and to transcribe it in a simple gesture. Painting, sculpture, and music suppose that the artist first goes through a stage of writing, or formulation on the canvas, or scoring, before the sublimation. But photography is an instant medium and Mézière uses it superbly, like a footbridge that leads us toward the natural brilliance of things.

Mézière is looking not for the ideal reality, but for the perfect illusion. "Every night I went to sleep hoping to wake up to discover the perfect sunrise, the luminous valley which could satisfy all my illusions. Treasures are always hidden, so why not look for them?"

Yet another paradox, the asceticism of the desert kindles the sensuality of Jean Mézière. Mézière is a sensualist, a hedonist who savors beauty. To his appetite for life, the desert offers only sand and pebbles, tortured terrain and ghost towns. Mézière makes the sensuality of aridity spring forth. From within this extreme deprivation, he dislodges nature's jubilation. It takes one who is hyper-sensual, hyper-sensitive, to capture the *passionate* force of these *desolate* landscapes.

On the undeniable reality of the desert, he juxtaposes the ingredients of a reality fabricated by man. A pink Cadillac planted at the edge of the desert like a big drop of candy … the side of a wall in a ghost town, showing a minuscule fresco in these infinite spaces … a fringe of cars thrust into the sand like beached ships … these are traces — as if man could only exist in the landscape symptomatically, as if civilization washed over it again with its dreams of conquest, leaving behind some anachronistic sediment. Mézière juggles these traces, showing superb *trompe-l'oeil* images and Magritte-like scenes. Who but Mézière could capture them, he whose vision takes its bearings not from the paths that man intended to trace but from the crossing paths where the poet, by verb and image, opens the paths rather than following them?

Mathias Schmitt

CYCLE

ECHO

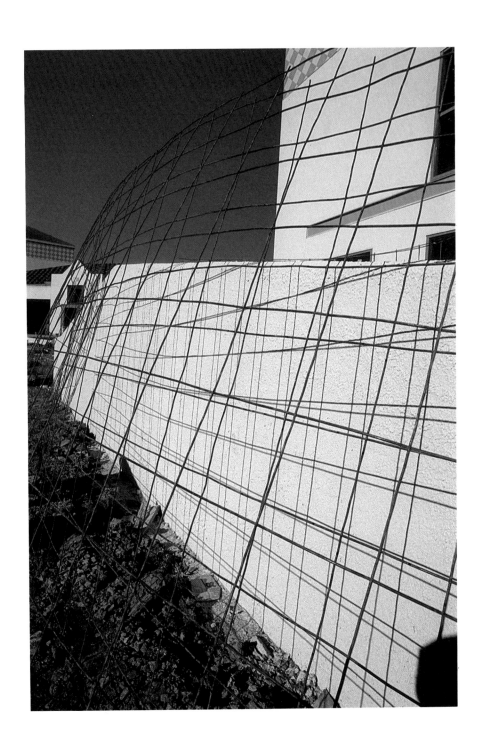

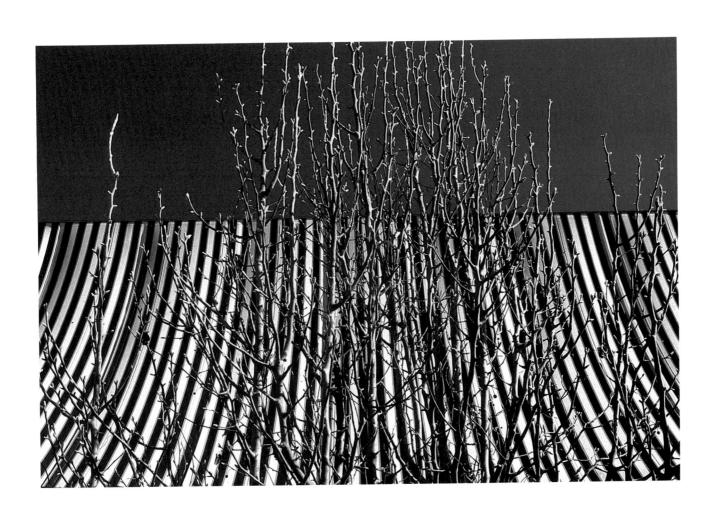

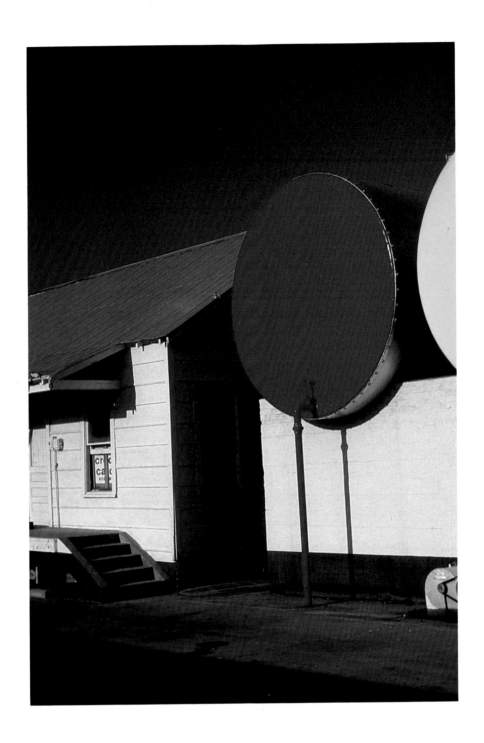

TRANSITION

TIME

SPACE

SEA

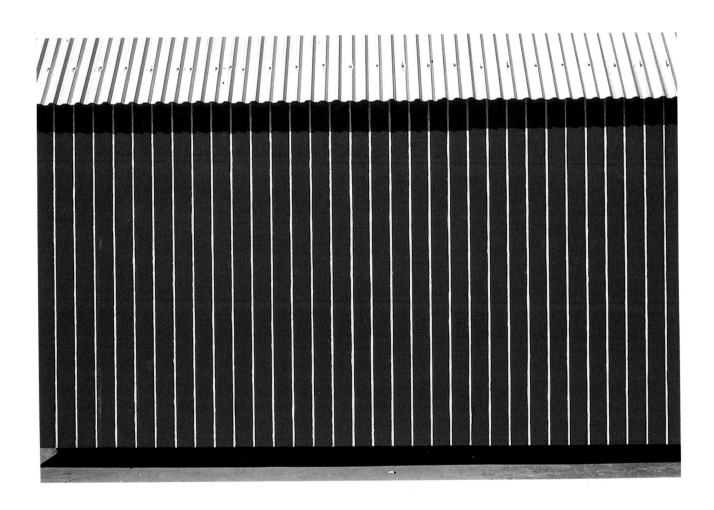

INDEX TO PHOTOGRAPHS

ACKNOWLEDGEMENTS

My thanks to Pete Kelly for his assistance on the trip west.

Also to the following establishments for their support:

Super Tex

Cameras Dallas

Polaroid Corporation,
Cambridge, Massachusetts

Hertz Dallas

BWC Photolab

the Taylor staff

143